SHILOH AND DANDE THE LION

CIARA L. HILL

Copyright © 2019 by Ciara L. Hill

All rights reserved. No part of this publication may be reproduced, distributed, or transmitted in any form or by any means, including photocopying, recording, or other electronic or mechanical methods, without the prior written permission of the copyright owner, except in the case of brief quotations embodied in critical reviews and certain other noncommercial uses permitted by copyright law.

Published by:
Lawton Classic Books
Bowie, Maryland 20716

Illustrated by: Christian Krabbe

Printed in the United States of America

PAPERBACK: 978-1-7341565-0-8
HARDBACK: 978-1-7341565-2-2
Ebook: 978-1-7341565-1-5

Library of Congress Control Number: 2019916937

www.ciaralhillbooks.com

This Book Belongs To

_____

Shiloh, my son, this book is dedicated to you. There is no greater legacy that I can leave behind for you than this book. I believe in you. Don't ever let anything stop you. I am proud of you, and I love you more than you will ever know.

To my husband and my family, thank you for believing in me and for never doubting my capabilities. Thank you for understanding my vision and giving me much needed advice and inspiration.

To all my readers: Let this book be a testament to the fact that you are beautiful, unique and special, in spite of whatever adversity you may face. Don't ever let anyone define who you are without your permission. Be brave and be courageous. And, most importantly, be yourself!

Today was Shiloh's first day at his new school. Shiloh was very nervous but determined to think positive.

"I'm going to find the courage to be myself. Good things are going to happen. I hope the other kids like me." Shiloh said to himself.

However, after school, Shiloh got back home, feeling sad. "Mom, I don't like my new school," Shiloh sighed. "The kids keep telling me that I am different; they kept talking about my brown skin."

"You are right," said Shiloh's mom. "You are different, but it's because there is only one of you. That's what makes you special. Everyone is not the same. The world would be boring if we all looked alike".

Shiloh's mom paused for a few seconds. Locking eyes with her son, she added, "Guess what else?"

"What, Mom?"

"You have a big job to do."

"What's that?" asked Shiloh.

"You have to show the whole world how amazing you are," replied Shiloh's mom. "Your Dad and I named you Shiloh because that means peace. It means you are in tune with who you are. It means you must always be yourself."

Shiloh wanted to do that. But he didn't know how. He did know he wanted to think about his Mom's words, so Shiloh decided to walk in his backyard.

While Shiloh was in his backyard, he noticed a pretty yellow flower. He pulled it from the ground and took it home for his mom. He knew how much she loved flowers.

At home, Shiloh held the flower delicately in his hands. He approached his mom and asked, "What is the name of this flower?"

"That flower is a beautiful dandelion," said Shiloh's mom. "Do you know what makes a dandelion flower unique?"

Shiloh considered the beautiful flower in his hands. "I know dandelion flowers are pretty," he said. "I know they have a nice yellow color, but I do not know what makes them unique."

His mom explained, "When you make a wish, dandelions help make it come true. Dandelions also help you overcome hard times."

Shiloh had no doubt his mom was very wise. After thinking about what she said, he looked around his room. Shiloh spotted his favorite stuffed animal: a beautiful lion, with colorful fur. He knew then and there he would name the stuffed animal "Dande the Lion."

Before bedtime that night, Shiloh's parents tucked him tightly under the covers.

"Goodnight, Shiloh," they said. "We love you very much. Remember to always dream big."

As Shiloh drifted off to sleep, he clutched Dande the Lion in his hand.

Shiloh then whispered "Dande the Lion, what do you see? Please help others understand me!"

And just like that, Shiloh began to dream.

SHILOH

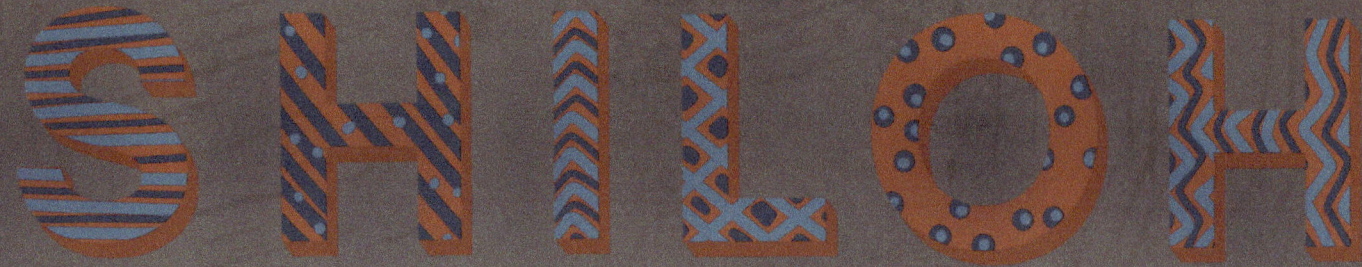

Before he knew it, he was on a beach. Shiloh could not believe it. Dande the Lion stood beside him, but this time, he was a real lion.

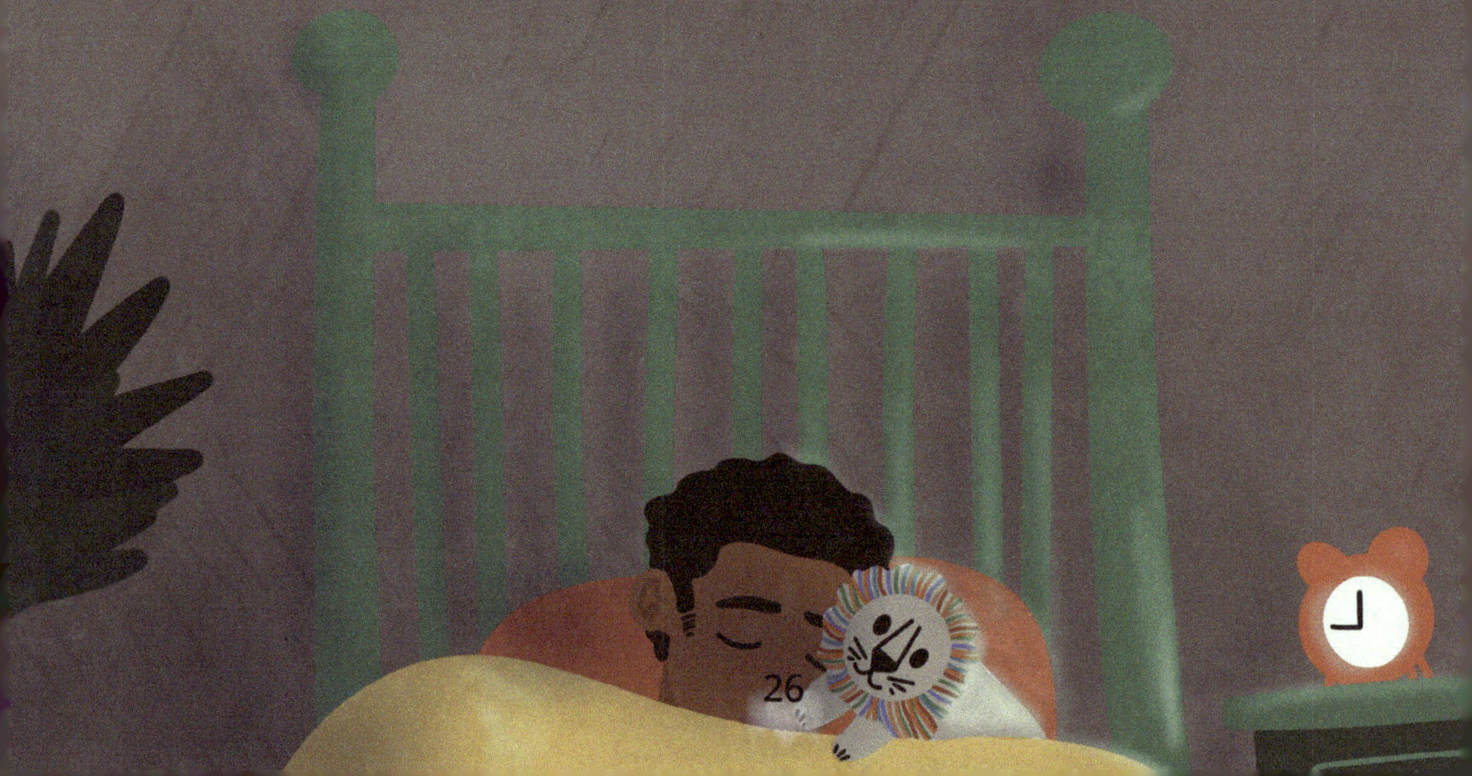

When he and Dande the Lion looked out at the sparkling water, they saw a mermaid and some seals.

"Wow!" said Shiloh. Who were all these wonderful creatures?

The mermaid's name was Birdie, and the seals called themselves the Stinky Crew.

When Birdie noticed Shiloh, she approached him with an expression of awe on her face. She took one hard look at him and said he was different from anything she had ever seen before.

"You don't belong here!" she cried.

The Stinky Crew agreed with Birdie. "You are smelly," they added, crinkling their noses at Shiloh.

A wave of sadness washed over Shiloh as he dug his toes into the sand.

Thankfully, Dande the Lion stepped in. He gazed at Birdie and the Stinky Crew with his deep lion eyes and said, "If you took the time to play with Shiloh, you might learn something."

The next thing Shiloh knew, Dande the Lion was taking him for a swim. He told Shiloh he wanted to show him how some of the sea creatures dealt with others who were not very nice.

The pair met a huge whale named Peewee. Shiloh and Dande the Lion rode on Peewee's back and moved swiftly through the water. Then Dande the Lion told Peewee what had happened to Shiloh. Peewee shared that he too was bullied at one point, because of his size.

But Peewee told Shiloh that he soon learned he was special. And when he realized nothing was wrong with his true self, he became much happier. Peewee offered a reassuring smile. He promised to show Shiloh something that only he could do, all because of his awesome size.

Before Shiloh could thank Peewee for his kindness, an octopus named Twinkle Toes pulled Shiloh and Dande the Lion right off the whale's back. Next to Twinkle Toes swam Birdie and the Stinky Crew.

They were dragged down to the deepest part of the ocean. Darkness surrounded them.

In the depths of the water, Shiloh heard splishing and splashing, babbling bubbles, and gurgling sounds. He and Dande the Lion felt slimy seaweed and fins from the ocean mammals.

Under the sea, they didn't care about their differences.

They were all a little scared, but they were all in this together.

Dande the Lion knew he still had to help Shiloh embrace the things that made him outstanding. He asked Peewee to show Shiloh what he had promised to do. So, Peewee showed Shiloh that because of his size, he was able to shed the most light.

Peewee made the deep, dark water bright enough for everyone to play.

While playing, the sea creatures were amazed at how fast Shiloh could swim. They also admired how nice he was to everyone, even though some of them had been mean to him.

When they swam back to shore, Twinkle Toes made everyone gather around his tentacles. He explained that he was often teased because of his strange shape.

But then, he showed the others how he could do tricks with his eight long arms. He showed them how even though he looked different than the others, he always had a lending hand to offer those in need. And that was not all, Twinkle Toes had three beating hearts!

He explained to the group how he used his hearts to show others how much he cared.

Shiloh turned thoughtfully to Twinkle Toes. He remembered Peewee's kindness and Dande the Lion's bravery. He also remembered his mother's wise words. He decided then and there he wanted to show the world that he too was special.

So, Shiloh whispered, "Dande the Lion, what do you see? Please help others understand me!"

Suddenly, Shiloh felt a change deep inside him. He then found the courage to express what he felt.

"I am different like you are different" continued Shiloh. "I am also unique and strong."

Once again, Shiloh thought of his mom and dad. "I am going to dream big like my parents taught me!" he cried. "I am curious. I love to be around people and animals. I am brown and proud!"

Birdie and the Stinky Crew nodded cleverly. Soon after Shiloh's speech, they swam away.

The Stinky Crew waded in silence for a moment. "When we were under the water, our physical features didn't matter," they said. "Shiloh was nice to everyone. Plus, he's an awesome swimmer."

"It was cool to see how everyone is different," added Birdie. "No one ever taught us to see past others' differences before."

The next thing they knew, Birdie and the Stinky Crew gathered everyone together. They wanted to apologize to Shiloh.

Shiloh was overjoyed—so much so, that he and his new friends immediately began celebrating.

During the celebration, he thanked his new friends. He also thanked Dande the Lion. He was very grateful to his old pal, who not only showed him other creatures' special traits but also gave him the courage to be himself.

When Shiloh woke up from his dream, he was ready for the day to begin.

"I know how to help others understand me now!" he announced. "With patience, kindness, and understanding, we can all accept others for who they are."

Shiloh stared at Dande the Lion, who had turned back into a stuffed animal. "My mom was right about being yourself," he said. "And so were you."

SHILOH

Shiloh could not wait to enjoy his true self.

Everything would be okay, as long as he had Dande the Lion by his side.